THE FASHION SET

THE ART OF THE FASHION SHOW

ROADS Publishing
19–22 Dame Street
Dublin 2
Ireland

www.roads.co

First published 2016

1

The Fashion Set

Text copyright
© ROADS Publishing
Design and layout copyright
© ROADS Publishing
Front cover image: Mary Katrantzou,
Autumn/Winter 2016, London
© JUSTIN TALLIS/AFP/Getty Images

Designed in Ireland by WorkGroup
Printed in Spain

British Library Cataloguing
in Publication Data
A catalogue record for this book is
available from the British Library

978-1-909399-83-9

THE FASHION SET

THE ART OF THE FASHION SHOW

Federico Poletti
with Giorgia Cantarini

ROADS

PUBLISHING

Contents

Foreword

Colin McDowell

A rare jewel requires a beautiful setting. A great house would not be so great if, instead of its smooth lawns and stately trees, it was surrounded by factories. A badly placed *autostrada* can forever destroy a view that had been enjoyed for centuries. Any object of beauty needs a setting as a frame to bring out its perfection.

Nowhere is that more true than in high fashion. Ready-to-Wear can, of course, look after itself. It is merely merchandise, to be bought cheaply, put on and forgotten. It is in no way harmed by being sent down a plain runway, worn by girls who walk like automatons, whose faces are not only blank but are frequently vacant – usually not, let me say, because they are necessarily stupid, but because the designer, stylist and choreographer have told them that they wish them to behave that way.

It is high fashion that creates a real fashion show, in which the surroundings, along with the music, pace and rhythm of the event, all work as a beautiful setting to make the clothes come alive and have meaning.

There are not many such occasions, and they mainly take place in Europe or the UK. American designers realise that they are selling 'stuff', not dreams, which is why their approach to the fashion show is entirely utilitarian. In the past fifty years, although designers like Ralph Lauren and Calvin Klein have produced marvellously romantic clothes, their shows have remained a vehicle to sell those clothes in the simplest and most direct way.

When we come to Europe, things change. In Milan, Dolce & Gabbana have created marvellous *mise-en-scènes* for their clothes, especially when their creativity has been stimulated by the culture of their beloved Sicily.

Dsquared2, on the other hand, use American blue-collar mythology and humour in order to get their message across, while Roberto Cavalli, with his operatic sets that create a tone of opulence, speaks to his audience of *luxe, calme et volupte.*

But we must turn to Paris for the really great runway moments, when clothes and surroundings work together so closely that the show is almost like watching a film or an opera. But it must be admitted that, even in Paris, such perfection is rare. Costs are high. Full theatrical rehearsals are usually required. Lighting and sound arrangements are complex. Whole days – even weeks – can be required to build the set.

For many seasons, the shows created by the late Alexander McQueen, together with those created by John Galliano at Christian Dior, were the highlight of Paris Fashion Week, although many preferred the more cerebral approach of Dries Van Noten, Rick Owens and Martin Margiela. Recently, Karl Lagerfeld at Chanel has created amazing *mise-en-scènes* for his shows, including settings based on an airport and a casino.

I am pleased that we have this book as a reference and record of an element of fashion that it would seem will be very limited in the future, as costs escalate and profits drop.

Colin McDowell is one of the most influential figures in the global fashion community. A long-time Chief Fashion Writer for *The Sunday Times Style*, and founder and creative director of the Fashion Fringe initiative, he has written more than twenty books on fashion and related subjects.

Fashion Shows to Remember

Diane Pernet

Reminiscing about the most memorable fashion presentations I've seen, one in particular stands out from the rest, as the adventure began even before the start of the actual show. It was when Dries Van Noten celebrated his fiftieth runway show in 2005 and invited over 500 guests, even organising transportation for everyone to reach the show, which was held outside of Paris. We arrived and entered a sort of airline hangar, a big industrial building with a foggy atmosphere where guests were enjoying drinks and little treats. Then, all at once – almost like magic – everyone was walking into the next room where there was one very long table, a table for 500 people, with one waiter each ... or at least it seemed that way. The waiters served simultaneously. It was like a Peter Greenaway film – totally orchestrated in the most elegant, surreal way. A delicious dinner was served and then once the table was cleared, the table itself became the runway and the show began. After the show, an iron shelf was lowered and on it was a gift for each guest: an autographed copy of Dries Van Noten's book documenting his fifty collections. It was trimmed in gold. Afterwards, cars took us all home to Paris. Even the photographers were treated to a wonderful buffet. That show stands out as having been totally magical.

Much longer ago, A.F. Vandevorst did a show that began with models sleeping on hospital beds, with timed hidden lights that signalled to them to get up and walk the runway. It was powerful and original and far surpassed the typical catwalks of 1999. Then, of course, every Alexander McQueen show was memorable. In 2002, there were real wolves walking inside the gothic settings of La Conciergerie in Paris, the old Palace of Justice. It was as scary as it was fascinating, especially with the mysterious atmosphere you can sense inside that historical building. One I also remember well was the Ice Queen in the Autumn/Winter show of 2003, who walked across a very high bridge with a strong wind blowing her very long dress.

Then, of course, there are the Maison Margiela shows, which are always strong and simple. One collection featured a white show and a black show, lit by candles, and one of the models' hair accidentally caught fire. Nothing too dramatic, just a little lost hair. Or the show that was held in a series of cafés, supposedly projecting the same film simultaneously at seven locations, but it wasn't actually in sync ... some of the people who had been at the café earlier in the day were still there. I remember one of them asking me, 'Is this a student designer?' I thought it was quite funny.

Then there were those amazing Jurgi Persoons shows where he had girls in Plexiglas boxes out in the freezing cold, lining the Quai Austerlitz – and again, cars brought us there because no one knew who he was at the time, but it was great. Or many of the old W&LT shows under Walter Van Beirendonck; one, I remember, was on the edge of Paris with a winter wonderland theme. When you arrived, the tent was a constructed igloo with no lights, only little fluorescent candles on the ground to lead you to the entryway, like the Hansel and Gretel fairy tale. The only problem was that when the show ended, all the fluorescent candles were gone because people had taken them on the way in, so it was really difficult to find your way out.

Not forgetting the decadent Westwood shows at the Grand Hotel when she was at the height of her career: a luxurious, old-world setting with girls lounging on sofas, just being extravagantly beautiful. Or John Galliano's elegant and romantic shows at the Jardins de Bagatelle, with amazing flowers and little vignettes which smelled as good as they looked.

There are so many shows that deserve to be remembered. However, everyone has a different perception of each, as we feel emotions in our own way and our emotions trace our memories. That's why I remember these specifically – because they made an impression on me. From setting to show, they are still incredibly clear in my mind.

Diane Pernet is an international fashion blogger and critic. She is the creator of the pioneering blog A Shaded View on Fashion (ASVOF) and the founder and director of fashion film festival A Shaded View on Fashion Film (ASVOFF).

Behind the Fashion Set: The Art of Storytelling

Federico Poletti

What is the secret of a memorable runway show?

Despite its long history, the fashion show is still the privileged means by which designers exhibit their creations. Ever since the first Italian fashion show, organised by Giovanni Battista Giorgini in 1951, the concept has radically changed, yet the aim is still the same: to create emotion around the garments in order to spark an alchemy that makes us dream about dressing ourselves in those clothes. The idea to record the most stunning fashion shows from the past several years came from the desire to research, document and create an archive of a part of fashion that is often neglected, one which creates a magical experience each season, starting from scratch and then becoming realised right before our eyes. Looking at the industry from this perspective can shine a different light on fashion and its very own language. While fashion shows used to be considered a selling mechanism, almost an extension of the trade show, they have evolved to become as much a part of the spectacle and branding as the clothes themselves. Planning and constructing the sets, lighting and catwalk can take anywhere from several days to six months to execute, and often involves teams of specialised workers. When done right, these shows are a theatrical expression of the brand's seasonal vision; captivating and charged with electricity and excitement. The goal is always to put on a show for buyers, top clients and the media that evokes a sense of wonderment, inspiration and creativity.

Thus, two new key professions have emerged in the fashion scene: the fashion show producer and the set designer. They both share the responsibility of making sure that the designer's message comes across as precisely and clearly as possible. The fashion show producer looks after every detail of a show, from how the models walk to the set, to the lights and the music, while the set designer is in charge of the scenography, which has to follow the designer's vision and aesthetic. In the last few years, *maisons* have been developing more and more sophisticated backdrops to their collections in order to create a unique atmosphere, complemented by lighting and props which play a crucial role in the success of the show. In essence, a fashion show is not so different from a theatrical performance, the only difference being that a fashion show does not usually last more than twelve minutes and needs to leave a strong emotional impact on the audience. Chanel and Louis Vuitton – to name just two – have animated their fashion shows with stunning sets, creating immersive experiences that challenge the boundaries of fantasy. Some designers, like Karl Lagerfeld, design and think of everything themselves, so the set designers and producers have to translate and manifest the designer's ideas. Other times, the set designer can develop visual pyrotechnics or add their own vision to contribute to the creation of the designer's story.

Alexander McQueen, Spring/Summer 1999

This book aims to show the importance of the creative process and the work behind the modern fashion show. It is also a chance to ponder the lesser-known creatives involved in making each fashion show a success. For example, who could forget Fendi showing on the Great Wall of China in 2007, under the creative direction of Karl Lagerfeld? Or again, at the hand of Lagerfeld, the creation of the Chanel Supermarket for his 2014 Autumn/Winter collection?

Having worked with top clients in the fashion business, fashion show producer and scenographer Etienne Russo established his own event and show production company, Villa Eugénie, in 1995. He started working with the then lesser-known 'Antwerp Six', and in particular with the now well-known Dries Van Noten, in addition to some prestigious brands such as Maison Margiela and Hermès. Based in Brussels, and having built upon his first work with Van Noten, Russo is now considered one of the most innovative and forward-thinking producers in the industry. His talent relies on his understanding of his clients' needs, which might range from understated to emotional. In an interview for *Dazed & Confused*, he said: 'Some people want to whisper it and some want to shout it out loud. Spectacle is not right for everybody. It's about doing the right thing, finding the right balance and doing things the right way.'

Amongst other important companies specialising in the construction of sets is Bureau Betak, founded by Alexandre de Betak, which collaborates with some of the biggest fashion houses, including Dior, Jason Wu, Diane von Furstenberg, Viktor & Rolf, and Rodarte. Bureau Betak develops each brand's visual identity and language, and communicates it through shows and events that are known to be moving, memorable and, most of all, newsworthy.

Overcoming boundaries and designing with 'no limits' is the philosophy of YO Fashion & Luxury Events, an agency that orchestrates events in the worlds of fashion, luxury, beauty, fine jewellery and watchmaking. YO produced the Fendi set for the Great Wall of China, as well as memorable shows for Céline, Karl Lagerfeld, Jean Paul Gaultier, Lanvin and Louis Vuitton, enchanting the attendees with such evocative

Dries Van Noten, Spring/Summer 2005

Dior, Spring/Summer 2007

elements as the Louis Vuitton Express, a handsome one-carriage train built especially for the Autumn/Winter 2012 show. The set transported the label back to its beginnings as a luggage company, with its working train, porters and women styled as travellers.

Another well-established Paris-based agency, La Mode en Images, is founded by director, photographer and event organiser Olivier Massart. La Mode en Images manages every aspect of the fashion event, from artistic design, through casting and technical support, to creating a ready-to-wear solution with a tailored edge. Although fashion remains the agency's primary focus, its service and expertise are valued in many other areas of the luxury and design industries, including perfume, cosmetics, fine jewellery and watches. They boast an array of top luxury clients, including John Galliano, Louis Vuitton, Valentino, Givenchy, Christian Dior and Balenciaga.

The fashion set design business is growing, as evidenced by the success of many more production agencies, like OBO, with offices in New York and London, Sun Design Group in Tokyo, established in 1967, and Gainsbury & Whiting, London, who work with some of the UK's most exciting designers, including the production of Alexander McQueen's shows for the last six seasons. Eyesight, founded in 2002, has produced shows for Yves Saint Laurent, Helmut Lang, Rick Owens, Chloé, Barbara Bui and, most recently, the 2011 Autumn/Winter menswear shows for Phillip Lim, Dior Homme, Raf Simons, and Victor & Rolf in Paris.

A different approach to fashion set creation is demonstrated by Miuccia Prada, whose style rejects preconceived notions and traditional expectations. She is always able to surprise her audience, thanks to a successful partnership with Dutch architect Rem Koolhaas. Koolhaas's research and design studio AMO has partnered with Prada for their catwalk shows since 2004, entering new territory season after season. For each collection, the brand occupies the Fondazione Prada space in Milan, presenting shows that push the boundaries of the traditional runway formula.

Fashion show producers work behind the scenes, collaborating directly with designers, contributing to making each show a unique experience, catapulting the audience into another world. The sets can take anywhere from three days to six months to execute, at times involving hundreds of craftsmen, all to create twelve minutes of magic which, at its finest, can make the fashion experience come alive. The best shows are a highly concentrated collision of theatre, emotion, explosiveness and, often, good old-fashioned spectacle. Against all odds, designers and scenographers strive to preserve and inspire a sense of wonder and enchantment.

When we talk about the fashion set itself, the goal is to express the voice of the *avant garde*; just as in the collection it anticipates, the watchwords are 'experimental' and 'new'. Because, in essence, there would be no environment – no set – without the inspiration and clothing, but at the same time, there wouldn't be any show without a proper set. Everything must be in line and coherent. The set, while closely linked to the inspiration of the collection, should not overpower it; rather it should help the viewer enter deeper and deeper into the world that he or she is observing.

We decided to create this book to capture and celebrate the expertise and hard work, both creative and practical, that go into producing fashion shows, and the feelings and excitement they elicit in their audiences. The goal was to create a record of a ten-year evolution across several creative fields – not just fashion – and present it from a different point of view. And so this book aims to put the spotlight on fashion shows that are all-too-often dismissed as banal or are not appreciated for what they truly are: real artistic performances, capable of arousing emotions and leaving an audience breathless.

These are emotions that my staff and I have had the pleasure of experiencing, as we examined image after image, each one surprising and curious, because, as you will see, witnessing these masterpieces is never boring. Each is a miniature world that has been carefully planned and constructed, only to suddenly vanish after just twelve spectacular minutes.

Federico Poletti is an established Italian editor and an independent fashion curator. Co-founder and Editor-in-Chief of manintown.com, he has written for *Huffington Post Italy*, *D la Repubblica*, *Modern Weekly*, *Vogue* and *Vanity Fair Italia*.

ALEXANDER MCQUEEN

Autumn/Winter 2006 Ready-to-Wear, Paris

McQueen's AW06 show, entitled 'Widows of Culloden', took inspiration from European culture and the designer's own heritage. The highlight of the show was a ghostly Kate Moss hologram, which was designed by Baillie Walsh and art directed by McQueen, using keystoning and distortion to trick the eye.

ALEXANDER MCQUEEN

Autumn/Winter 2014 Ready-to-Wear, Paris

In showcasing this collection of trapeze-shaped silhouettes and swinging hems, creative director Sarah Burton's inspiration was the concept of 'Wild Beauty'. Upon a mossy surface covered with thousands of heather plants, models walked through a mysterious, moonlit space as if they were walking upon real earth. 'I wanted to see the woman's face again,' said Burton, 'free her a bit, touch her, feel her.'

ALEXANDER WANG

Spring/Summer 2016 Ready-to-Wear, New York

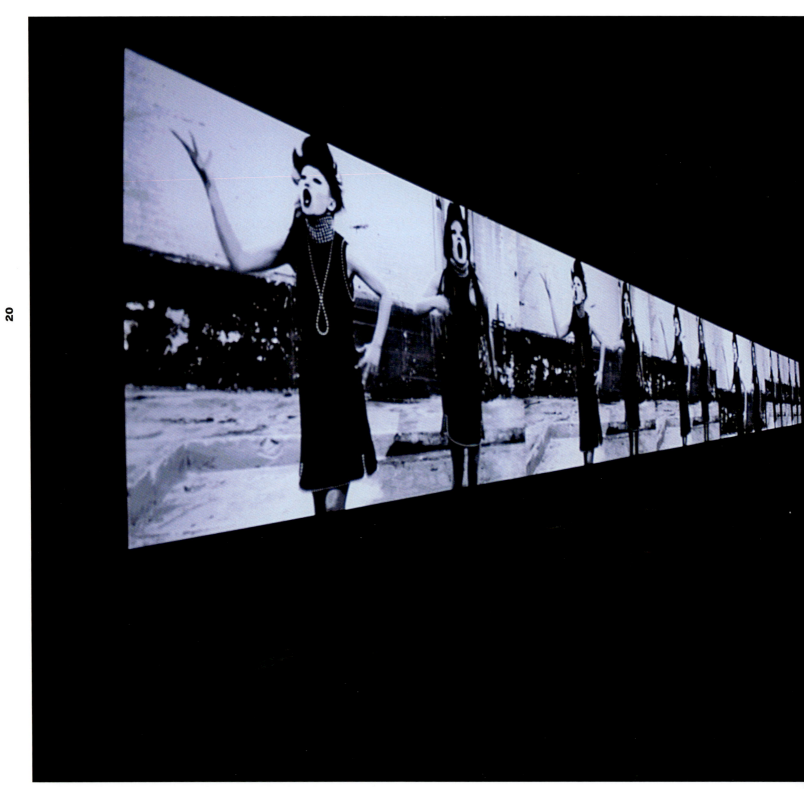

This show marked the tenth anniversary of the Alexander Wang brand in a suitably celebratory fashion. The collection was a return to Wang's streetwise roots, a concentration of all the sports luxe elements that he made his own. After the models took their finale spin in a flurry of silver confetti, a long screen the length of the catwalk played a video montage of the designer's impressive ten-year journey with his eponymous label.

This show took place at Moynihan Station in New York City, but the set carried the viewer to a tropical island by surrounding the stage with palm trees and a soundtrack that featured bird calls and luau music. The collection embodied a colourful and feminine kaleidoscope of beach florals, retro frills, rock 'n' roll and boho-chic. Models paraded between the palm trees as if they had come directly from the beach, their outfits completed with socks and sandals.

ANNA SUI

Spring/Summer 2016 Ready-to-Wear, New York

ANTONIO MARRAS

Autumn/Winter 2005 Ready-to-Wear, Milan

This Antonio Marras show was dedicated to the life of Tina Modotti – an Italian emigrant photographer and anti-fascist militant in the international communist movement who was exiled and persecuted for her work. The setting catapulted the viewer into another era – rural Mexico during the turbulent 1920s. Bathed in a soft light, the models sat on rocks behind a thin fabric, as if they were painted on the canvas itself. The show's concept was developed by Paolo Bazzani, founder of Paolo Bazzani Studio, which focuses on graphic art projects and art direction for the fashion industry.

ANYA HINDMARCH

Spring/Summer 2016 Ready-to-Wear, London

This collection, a continuation of Hindmarch's inventive use of pattern, was shown in a dizzying mirrored set that initially disguised the fact that the designer's tongue was firmly in cheek. The seemingly abstract pieces dazzled from every angle in the futuristic kaleidoscope, but as they settled into the scenography, the audience came to recognise the branding of UK high-street mainstays within the patterns. The graphics of shops such as WH Smith, Boots and Mothercare were incorporated within the choreographed scene in a manner that balanced nostalgia and wonder – transforming the most familiar branding into something modern, rhythmic and luxurious.

BOSS

Autumn/Winter 2014 Ready-to-Wear, New York

The German headquarters of Hugo Boss served as the source of inspiration for the future of the brand's womenswear line. The setting created a world where modernism and architecture coexist with nature, an elegant and tidy environment that was underlined by the colour scheme: light-grey buildings, green bushes and white flowers. Reflections of modernist buildings were surrounded by elegant greenery on this stunning stage, developed and executed by Bureau Betak.

The concept of Céline's AW08 show was 'Waiting Moment', and the power of anticipation. Production designers YO Fashion & Luxury Events created a special set at Espace Éphémère, its black runway adorned with a long curving neon light that kept everyone guessing as they waited for the show to start. This deceptively simple device captivated an increasingly excited audience, prefiguring a collection of fluid pieces in white, dove greys and black, punctuated with the odd burst of colour.

This season, in the middle of the Grand Palais, models emerged from a huge barn full of straw. In this collection, Karl Lagerfeld wanted to present fashion at its essence, working wonders with the use of simple, natural materials. The models literally romped in the hay wearing pieces that reflected the rural theme; aprons, clogs and ribbons all featured, moulded to fit Chanel's signature style. Musician Lily Allen rose from the floor on a straw-filled podium for a suprise performance, creating the impression of a glamorous country hoedown.

CHANEL

Spring/Summer 2010 Ready-to-Wear, Paris

CHANEL

Autumn/Winter 2010 Couture, Paris

For the AW10 Couture catwalk, Lagerfeld wanted to portray opulence, enhancing the extravagant setting of the Grand Palais with the installation of a giant golden lion statue, a nod to Coco Chanel's astrological sign. Models took to the runway through the enormous pearl beneath the lion's paw and encircled the stately figure, which, at nearly 12 metres tall, took thirty sculptors over three months to construct.

CHANEL

Spring/Summer 2011 Ready-to-Wear, Paris

Taking inspiration from the film *Last Year at Marienbad*, Lagerfeld outfitted the Grand Palais to mirror one of the film's most famous scenes. An incredibly surreal setting, including a monochrome ornamental garden complete with fountains, was lit by the greenhouse-style glass ceiling while a full live orchestra of eighty musicians played romantic arrangements of music by Björk, the Verve and John '007' Barry as the show's soundtrack.

Lagerfeld transformed the Grand Palais into a pearlescent white underwater fantasy world to reflect Chanel's collection of ruffled dresses, iridescent glowing woven jackets and pink pearl *pochettes* in the shape of shells. White coral, seashells and seahorses in giant proportions decked out the runway, with a musical accompaniment by Florence Welch, who appeared on a half-shell to perform her song 'What the Water Gave Me'.

CHANEL

Spring/Summer 2012 Ready-to-Wear, Paris

CHANEL

Pre-Autumn 2012, Paris

In the Galerie Courbe of the Grand Palais, Lagerfeld recreated a little piece of India, despite having never visited the country. His Pre-Autumn 2012 collection, titled 'Paris-Bombay', took inspiration from the notion of the extravagant life of India's privileged class. Showing a collection in shades of fuchsia, snowy white, gold and silver, the models walked around dining tables set with candelabras and sweets for high tea, while a Chanel-emblazoned toy steam train carried crystal decanters of a signature drink to guests.

CHANEL

Autumn/Winter 2012 Ready-to-Wear, Paris

Inspired by nature and an exhibition of Czech Cubism he visited while in Prague, Lagerfeld outfitted the floor of the Grand Palais with giant geometric amethyst and crystal stalagmites in brooding black and grey. Mirroring the collection, which included pieces and footwear lavishly embellished with crystal hems and trim, he also made colourful nods to the palette of Czech painter Emil Filla's 1934 oil painting *Zátiší s dýmkou* (*Still Life with Pipe*).

CHANEL

Spring/Summer 2013 Ready-to-Wear, Paris

Fascinated with the modern architectural structures of wind turbines and solar panels, Lagerfeld recreated them onstage for this homage to natural forms of energy. 'Energy is the most important thing in life,' he said, 'the rest comes later.' This towering set – and even bigger message – went with a collection of A-line silhouettes, boleros, dressy pieces appliqued with flowers, and chiffon cut-out dresses, which, although sweet, similarly communicated a love of lightness, scale, nature and technology.

For this collection, the *maison* installed a massive rotating globe right in the centre of the Grand Palais space, darkened as if night had fallen. Likewise, the collection reflected the night – dark and glittering metallic-thread tweeds shone through a deep palette, while monochrome flowers embellished the show's final pieces. The massive globe was marked with branded flags representing Chanel's worldwide retail presence.

CHANEL

Autumn/Winter 2013 Ready-to-Wear, Paris

CHANEL

Autumn/Winter 2013 Couture, Paris

Transforming the Grand Palais into a dilapidated post-apocalyptic theatre in ruins, Lagerfeld showcased his Couture collection among a crumbling stage, scattered rubble and broken fold-down chairs. The tattered curtains rose to reveal a backdrop of a futuristic city – the old world clashing with the new to great effect – symbolising how the old traditions of the *maison* were being combined with new technologies to create something spectacular.

As if overnight, a vast Pop Art supermarket sprang up in the Grand Palais, saturated with a very different kind of Chanel merchandise. The shelves groaned under the weight of everyday and decidedly unglamorous products, specially packaged in bright colours and emblazoned with the Chanel logo: breakfast cereals, doormats, black cotton buds, a chainsaw with a real Chanel chain. In the end, the set was a scene of both celebration and satire. Upon the store's 'closing', spectators were invited to help themselves to the fresh produce, whereupon a swarm of well-heeled looters descended, each grasping for their own piece of the Chanel *supermarché*.

CHANEL

Spring/Summer 2015 Couture, Paris

Spring was in the air at Chanel's SS15 Couture show. Paper flowers and plants of all sizes covered the Grand Palais floor, linked to a motorised system which caused them to burst into bloom at the spray of invisible water from a watering can. It took over six months to construct the 300 origami paper flowers that covered the stage. Lagerfeld demonstrated attitude with bare midriffs, slouchy skirts and oversized Edwardian hats, furthering Chanel's effort for constant, but thought-provoking, reinvention.

This Chanel collection began with the entrance of a number of celebrities, including Kristen Stewart and Julianne Moore. These famous guests and their escorts seated themselves around a number of large roulette tables that took up the centre of the room, and once the gambling started, the models entered the casino, with harshly cut hairstyles matching sharp tailoring and clean lines. The set began with pale two-piece suits and moved towards coloured statement dresses that pulled the focus away from the idling celebrities and placed it firmly on the clothes. At the close of the show, the featured guests stood to applaud Karl Lagerfeld before exiting the room arm-in-arm.

CHANEL

Autumn/Winter 2015 Couture, Paris

CHANEL

Spring/Summer 2016 Ready-to-Wear, Paris

AEROPORT PARIS CAMBON

CHANEL AIRLINES

DEPARTURES ✈

FLIGHT	To		GATE	TIME	FLIGHT	To		GATE	TIME
				10:58					
031	ROME	LAST CALL	07	11:00	035	SHANGHAI	ON TIME	09	11:30
719	SINGAPORE	BOARDING	06	11:07	448	NEW YORK	ON TIME	04	11:35
381	DUBAI	ON TIME	01	11:15	278	MOSCOW	ON TIME	10	11:43
475	DALLAS	ON TIME	08	11:24	339	LONDON	ON TIME	02	11:50
019	SALZBURG	ON TIME	02	11:28	182	TOKYO	ON TIME	03	11:55

CHANEL AIRLINES

14

CHANEL AIRLINES

Outdoing himself yet again, Lagerfeld installed a huge airport terminal for Chanel Airlines in the Grand Palais. The audience was invited into a busy set complete with waiting areas, a destination board, luggage carts and boarding gates. Airport staff worked at the check-in desks, while models played the role of first-class travellers, pulling wheeled suitcases behind them and sporting elegant sunglasses. Bright patterns, ambient music and visor-like make-up were the order of the day.

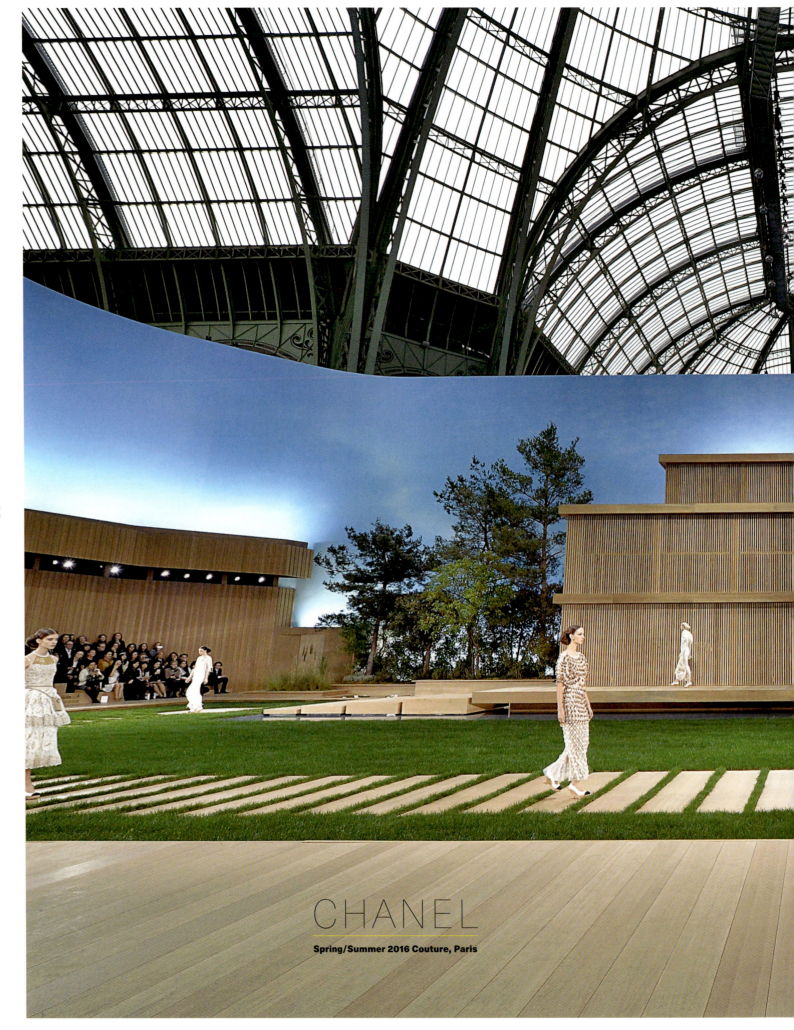

CHANEL

Spring/Summer 2016 Couture, Paris

From a minimalist three-storey wooden pavilion, zen-like models emerged as if from a doll's house, walking a path that encircled a grassy field and small pond. With open spaces and a simulated blue sky, the mood was meditative and nature-oriented, which extended to the collection. Fabrics were light and focused on shades of beige, with subtle details such as birds and bees adorning many pieces. 'This is high-fashion ecology,' Lagerfeld stated.

Combining Christian Dior's personal love of the countryside and creative director Raf Simons' idea of rebirth, the *maison* showed this collection in Paris's Tuileries Garden. Models walked between neatly trimmed grassy knolls topped with barren trees, displaying beautifully tailored peplum shapes and layered dresses, proving that Simons, with his second collection, had earned his place at Dior.

DIOR

Spring/Summer 2013 Couture, Paris

For Raf Simons' third collection for Dior, we found ourselves deep down the rabbit hole. His take on 'Alice's Garden' was constructed in a tent in the garden of the Musée Rodin, where a thick canopy of flowers – lianas, orchids and wisteria, real and fake – fell from stark metal scaffolding. The result was at once romantic and fresh, Simons explained: 'I wanted to feel that you wouldn't know quite where these women were coming from and where they were going to, that they exist in a new place of change and possibility.' This lush but playful hanging garden was symbolic of Simons' developing role in the *maison*, and the conflict between tradition and modernity, the maximalist and the minimalist.

DIOR

Spring/Summer 2014 Ready-to-Wear, Paris

DIOR

Autumn/Winter 2014 Couture, Paris

Held at one of the *maison*'s favourite locations, the Musée Rodin, Raf Simons presented a walk through history, from an eighteenth-century French Court through the Edwardian period to modern times. The set was circular with curved walls covered with thousands of luscious white orchids, and models emerged from various entrances. The pale colours, gentle music and soft cuts created a calm and serene atmosphere in the historic museum setting.

DIOR

Spring/Summer 2015 Couture, Paris

In thinking about modernity, Raf Simons delved
into the past and combined references from
French history with uniforms from such diverse
occupations as pilots, astronauts and schoolgirls.
His audience sat in a circle beneath an octagonal
mirrored dome while models walked atop a pink
carpet and among a complex maze of industrial
metal scaffolding and staircases.

DIOR

Autumn/Winter 2015 Couture, Paris

For this collection, Simons was inspired by the Flemish masters, creating outfits that displayed a classic elegance underlined by loose, flowing cuts and nude make-up. The setting itself was a Perspex palace: panels of Pointillist plastic hung above a purple catwalk dotted with coloured spheres. The contrast between the futuristic setting and the purity of the collection made for a sensational show.

72

Before this show for Dior Homme, Kris Van Assche insisted that there would be no historical references in the collection, opting instead for the term 'techno-sartorial'. The black curtains were raised to reveal a long line of chairs in single file down a grey tiled runway occupied by members of a live orchestra, who proceeded to perform the work of French musician Koudlam as the models took to the catwalk. This marriage of old and new was reflected in Van Assche's modern take on classic formal menswear: models were adorned in tweed suits and tuxedos decorated with oversized lapel pins, alongside ironically sporty sneakers and baseball caps.

With the French Riviera as a backdrop, Simons showed his Cruise collection at Pierre Cardin's famous Palais Bulles, a maze-like structure of giant rounded pods and portholes. Set on the side of a cliff near Cannes, just days before the opening of the famed film festival, the Dior collection reflected its stunning setting with pieces that were 'playful, sweet … childish, almost,' according to Simons.

DIOR

2016 Cruise, Théoule-sur-Mer

Calling this collection 'In All Disorder, A Secret Order', Van Assche presented a buttoned-up array of contemporary looks, including streetwear staples accented in orange, inspired by a contemporary urban garden. Models walked in an immaculate space, among 2,000 white rose bushes emerging from the parquet floor. The angular pattern of the garden and the subversive yet exquisitely controlled elements of Van Assche's collection were reflected in a giant tilted mirror.

DIOR

Spring/Summer 2016 Homme, Paris

For this show, Dior built a towering landscape of 300,000 blooming blue delphinium flowers in the Cour Carrée outside the Louvre Museum. Realised by set designer Alexandre de Betak, guests were seated inside as models curved around a smaller indoor hill of blossoms. Painted blue cranes hovered overhead providing lighting. Simons' mission statement for this collection was 'to simplify and concentrate on a line that expresses an idea of femininity, fragility and sensitivity, without sacrificing strength and impact'.

DIOR

Spring/Summer 2016 Ready-to-Wear, Paris

Influenced by subcultures such as punk, skate, new wave and emo, Dior Homme designer Kris Van Assche wanted to create a collection that would morph past and present together without dipping into nostalgia. Sullen models traced a rectangular runway laid down between neon-lined skate ramps, while an abstract film featuring the models themselves played in the background. Black fingernails, red tartan, shaggy haircuts and beanie hats were visible, with 1980s band Soft Cell providing the soundtrack. The effect was a show that paid homage to past subcultures while updating them for a modern audience.

The set for Domenico Dolce and Stefano Gabbana's menswear collection this season was all about their love for Sicily. The religiosity of the south of Italy was evident in the altar at the entrance to the catwalk, adorned with floral bouquets and showing the image of the Madonna and Jesus. The mood was enhanced by dim lighting and incense hanging in the air, evoking a Caravaggio painting in the *chiaroscuro* style. Traditional family values and the greatest love of all, that between a mother and her child, were expressed in the collection, the inspiration for which was 'devotion'.

DOLCE & GABBANA

Autumn/Winter 2013 Menswear Milan

Autumn/Winter 2012 Ready-to-Wear, Paris

84

Dries Van Noten called upon five painters to studiously recreate the work of typographer Job Wouters (aka Letman) and Dutch artist Gijs Frieling along a 30-metre wall while models marched down the runway. The appearance of a space under construction brought a surreal sense of immediacy to the show, while the sombre music was at once relaxing and engaging. The giant, brightly coloured murals reflected the collection's printed suits, jackets and typography-adorned shirts.

Dries Van Noten's spring collection was inspired both by John Everett Millais's *Ophelia* and by Shakespeare's *A Midsummer Night's Dream*, and the romantic mood was achieved with soft, dreamy spot-lighting emulating the sunlight through trees. A dense, moss-like carpet created specially by Argentinean artist Alexandra Kehayoglou suggested a deep forest floor in place of a runway, and the soundtrack evoked the sounds of the woodlands. The hazy, fairy-tale atmosphere welcomed light fabrics and glittering elements, and at the finale the models sat on the runway in serene contentment, a perfect image to encapsulate the designer's vision of 'a girl who loves the full moon but also the sunlight'.

Dsquared2 twins Dean and Dan Caten were inspired by James Dean and his style for this menswear collection, pondering what the icon may have worn if his plane crashed on a tropical island. The suitably imaginative set by Stefano Grossi was complete with luxuriant vegetation and the relic of a 1950s-style plane, and the show opened with a model showering beneath one of the working waterfalls. The collection embraced this high-concept theme, with tropical motifs, Bermuda shorts, and, of course, their take on James Dean's famous red leather jacket.

DSQUARED2

Spring/Summer 2014 Menswear, Milan

This show opened with a model being dragged down the runway in a straitjacket, so there was no confusing the overt imagery of a prison at Dsquared2's show. Models wore orange coveralls and institutional uniforms, and stood imposingly against the metal bars of a jailhouse setting. Each model navigated a cold set of staircases and cells before posing aggressively at the end of a runway lit up by searchlights. Punching bags, weightlifting benches and the sound of police sirens completed the scene.

DSQUARED2

Autumn/Winter 2014 Menswear, Milan

ELIE SAAB

Spring/Summer 2016 Couture, Paris

For this collection, Elie Saab envisioned an Englishwoman visiting early-twentieth-century India. The set was made up of a jungle backdrop, earth-coloured flooring and tropical plants, while the soundtrack featured low beats with animalistic roars. The clothing combined pale Edwardian lace with jewelled headpieces and traditional Indian drapings. Sheer, delicate fabrics were contrasted with hardy jungle boots and satchels, creating an ambience of both elegance and exploration. The programme invited the audience to 'Enter India', and the immersive set and clothing created an opulent and imperialistic world set against a wild background.

ERDEM

Spring/Summer 2013 Ready-to-Wear, London

The inspiration for this collection was the work of Zenna Henderson, a 1960s sci-fi writer who created a race known as 'The People' – humanoids from another planet who are forced to move to Earth from their home world. The set was a massive geodesic dome made up of pale triangles with a wooden framework, a structure that was as otherworldly as the inspiration for the collection. Pastels contrasted with vibrant neons, creating an awkward colour palette that matched the theme of aliens trying to fit into a new world.

ERMENEGILDO ZEGNA

Autumn/Winter 2015 Couture, Milan

This Ermenegildo Zegna set recreated a lush forest, from the mounds of earth to the sounds of chirping birds and distant thunder. Representing the need for sustainability and the importance of preserving nature, Stefano Pilati also used recycled plastic in his coat designs, and models walked along an earth-coloured runway to the prophetic 1968 anthem 'All Along The Watchtower'.

ETRO

Spring/Summer 2016 Menswear, Milan

Designer Kean Etro reflected on the concept of
the egg for his collection, and how it represents
the primordial embryo of life before the split into
either male or female. The fascination with the egg
extended to the shape of the runway, which was
oval, and a series of gaping, abandoned rooms
were projected onto the changing backdrop.
Complementing the aboriginal influences on the
collection was a soundtrack of didgeridoo music,
an instrument that the designer himself plays.

This staggering achievement, designed by YO Fashion & Luxury Events, was a watershed moment in fashion set production. Working with Karl Lagerfeld, the team created a truly unique catwalk on a stretch of the ancient Great Wall of China, on which eighty-eight models walked against the backdrop of the stunning Guangou Valley. Lagerfeld said he wanted to bring the West to the East, and so he played with the sacred symbol of the circle to express harmony between these two very different cultures. At an estimated cost of $10 million, and a year in the making, it was certainly a strong statement as to the emerging importance of China for the luxury goods and fashion industries.

FENDI

Spring/Summer 2008 Ready-to-Wear, Juyongguan

FENDI

Spring/Summer 2013 Ready-to-Wear, Milan

This show was staged in the Fondazione Arnaldo Pomodoro, the permanent Milanese headquarters of the *maison*. The walls of the playfully surreal set were lined with geometric stripes, while large silver balloons hung above the catwalk, which gave the impression of sitting inside a spaceship. The contrast between the soft, lean, natural wood and the metallic spheres created a futuristic sci-fi ambience for a minimalist collection majestically orchestrated by Karl Lagerfeld and Silvia Venturini Fendi.

GIVENCHY

Autumn/Winter 2014 Menswear, Paris

This Givenchy menswear collection was inspired by Riccardo Tisci's childhood love of basketball combined with the sobriety of the Bauhaus movement. The runway was a neon-lined basketball court enclosed in circular railings, and the collection displayed hints of materials and designs used in the sport itself. Furs and oversized tailoring lent the clothing an animalistic vibe that was paired with slicked-back hairstyles.

Showing his collection in New York on 11 September, the fourteenth anniversary of the 9/11 terrorist attacks, Riccardo Tisci's show shone with grace and sensitivity, just like the beacons of light emanating from the former World Trade Centre site that night. Tisci teamed up with friend and performance artist Marina Abramović who created the set from recycled materials. A choreographed ritual of slowed-down movements represented a moment of pause as guests took in the glow of the sunset over the Hudson River at New York's Pier 26. Tisci's skilful collection, as well as his thoughtful approach to a date heavy with meaning, was a beautiful meditation on mourning, reflecting and living.

GIVENCHY

Spring/Summer 2016 Ready-to-Wear, New York

HENRIK VIBSKOV

Spring/Summer 2015 Ready-to-Wear, Copenhagen

Entitled 'The Brick Sticky Fingers', this evocative Henrik Vibskov show involved the installation of a pool in the centre of a huge industrial warehouse. Members of the Norwegian National Ballet entered the pool, and their gentle movements slowly developed into dramatic whipping motions, while the models walked around them in a collection of 3D sweaters, knitted patterns and stunning cut-outs, which were inspired by cement mixers, construction sites, bricks, and swimming pools. In the end, the dancers took to the runway alongside the models for a spectacular finale.

'The Messy Massage Class', Vibskov's AW15 catwalk, was a performance on the spectrum between fashion presentation and art installation. Guests were seated by 'Team VIBS' attendants in white shirts while the 20-metre set remained hidden behind a brown and pink curtain. The curtain finally opened to reveal 400 gloves suspended over participants on covered stretchers, which began to move hypnotically as the models marched onto the catwalk to a vocalist accompaniment.

HENRIK VIBSKOV

Autumn/Winter 2015 Ready-to-Wear, Copenhagen

HUNTER ORIGINAL

Autumn/Winter 2015 Ready-to-Wear, London

The wild Highlands of Scotland, founding place of
Hunter, inspired this collection, where the romantic,
rugged landscape was reimagined in an urban
industrial space to interpret the brand's heritage in
a modern context. Environmental features such as
rocks, heather and lichens were reflected in the
collection itself, with textures and colour palettes
inspired by the Scottish Glens appearing on
the runway. The set featured geometric catwalks
surrounded by working waterfalls, which crossed
the runway to fill a pool at the centre of the stage.

IRIS VAN HERPEN

Autumn/Winter 2014 Ready-to-Wear, Paris

With this show, titled 'Biopiracy', Iris van Herpen showed a dramatic but unsettling homage to the human genome by suspending three models from the ceiling in clear plastic bags. As the air was slowly sucked out of the bags, the models wriggled around like tadpoles, while the other models marched down the runway below wearing sleek, futuristic outfits and 3D-printed pieces.

KENZO

Autumn/Winter 2011 Ready-to-Wear, Paris

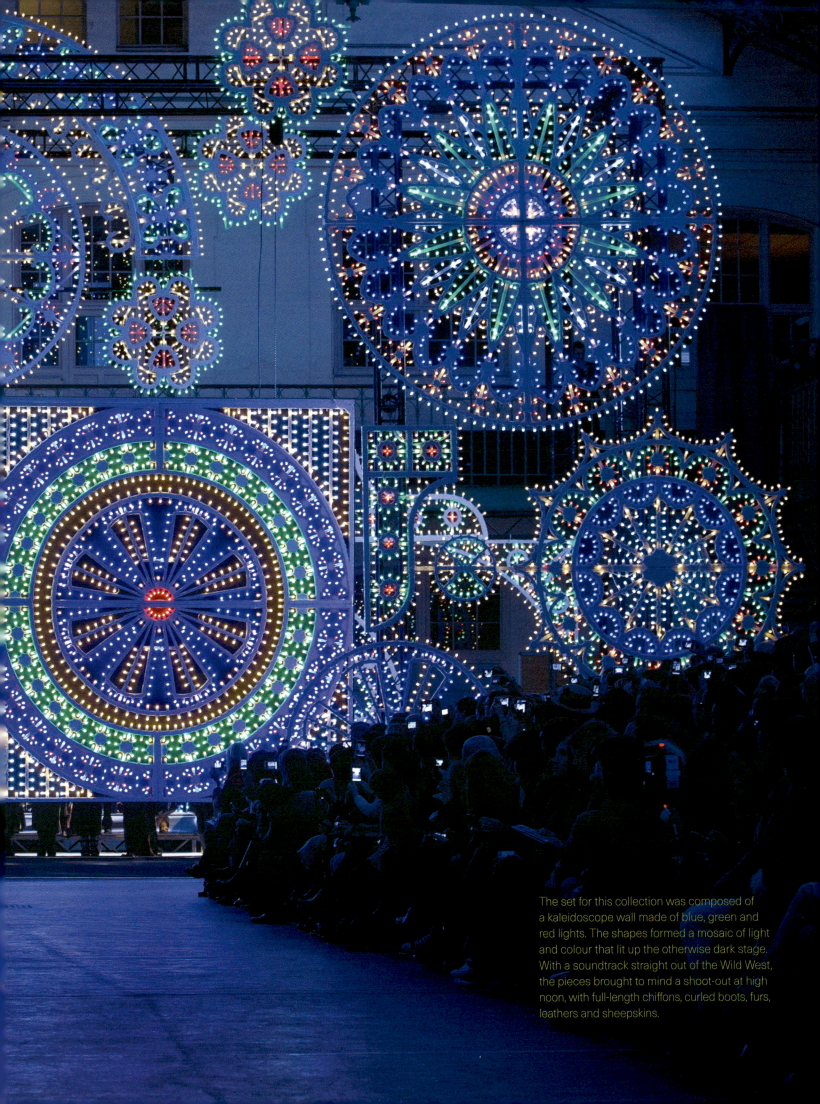

The set for this collection was composed of a kaleidoscope wall made of blue, green and red lights. The shapes formed a mosaic of light and colour that lit up the otherwise dark stage. With a soundtrack straight out of the Wild West, the pieces brought to mind a shoot-out at high noon, with full-length chiffons, curled boots, furs, leathers and sheepskins.

The importance of protecting our oceans and water resources was the message at this Kenzo show in Paris, announcing the label's partnership with a marine conservation charity. The models appeared from behind a wall of rain that was pouring down from the ceiling. In the centre, speakers pulsated with drops of water as models circled, wearing outfits featuring fish symbols, goggle-like sunglasses and rippling waves.

KENZO

Spring/Summer 2014 Ready-to-Wear, Paris

In discussing the source of inspiration for this collection, Lanvin designer Alber Elbaz described his birth country of Morocco as 'a country of contradictions'. Models marched down an alternately lit and shaded runway made of traditionally patterned Moroccan tiles. The collection paid tribute to the Sahara, with tasselled boots, shaggy goat-hair-trimmed coats and wraps, gold accessories and Berber stripes.

LANVIN

Autumn/Winter 2015 Ready-to-Wear, Paris

Sugar-sweet and playful as a little girl's paradise, Marc Jacobs' carousel-themed runway show provided the perfect backdrop to his just-as-saccharine collection of perforated faille skirt suits, daisy eyelet lace dresses and puffed skirts in retro silhouettes adorned with candy-pastel-coloured wisps of feathers. In this dreamy Vuitton wonderland, the models posed on white horses while a music box played throughout.

LOUIS VUITTON

Spring/Summer 2012 Ready-to-Wear, Paris

For this collection, Marc Jacobs took his audience back in time to the golden age of travel, transforming the runway space into a vintage train station where a real old-fashioned steam engine entered on a sunken track. Models dressed as passengers disembarked and circled the platform, decked out in jewel-encrusted fur coats, feather-topped hats and elbow-length leather gloves, in an homage to the brand's travel roots, as uniformed porters followed carrying their bags.

LOUIS VUITTON

Autumn/Winter 2012 Ready-to-Wear, Paris

LOUIS VUITTON

Autumn/Winter 2012 Menswear, Paris

For this show, under the direction of Kim Jones, the set designer placed an enormous globe above the runway. The globe mirrored the models walking below, reflecting the catwalk in a rounded, distorted perspective. The show was live-streamed online, and coats and bags were the collection's key pieces.

Vuitton's SS13 show was a punch of graphic vibrancy, as Jacobs channelled the 1960s in his collection. In pairs, models in co-ordinated outfits descended four escalators, delivered as if from the sky onto a white and yellow checked runway. Jacobs collaborated with artist Daniel Buren on the set design, and in fact Buren's famous installation *Les Deux Plateaux* inspired the collection's three distinct hem lengths. The show was a perfectly timed and executed operation, ripe with playful surprises for the audience, as the collection offered a fresh take on mod fashion, enriched with almost invisible details, such as stacked sequins and chequered velvet.

LOUIS VUITTON

Autumn/Winter 2013 Menswear, Paris

Journeying into the Kingdom of Bhutan, artistic
director Kim Jones sent models down a
mirrored runway against a backdrop of an icy
mountain. The collection was suitably wintry,
with furs and leathers suitable for a high-fashion
trip to the Himalayas.

LOUIS VUITTON

Spring/Summer 2014 Ready-to-Wear, Paris

Spring 2014 marked the final collection for Marc Jacobs after sixteen years as creative director at Louis Vuitton, and he dedicated the season to the women who had touched him and 'the showgirl in every one of them'. With a collection of nearly all black garments, including sheer embellished bodysuits, feathered hats and sequined jackets, the models circled an installation made up of many of the elements that made Jacobs' showmanship so famous: a water fountain, a carousel and an escalator, all painted a deep, sombre black over a plush midnight carpet.

Nicolas Ghesquière discovered the Bob and Dolores Hope Estate on his first trip to Palm Springs, fifteen years prior to this spectacular show. Designed by one of America's most influential and forward-thinking architects, John Lautner, the house is a space-age interjection in the desert hills – a perfect setting for Ghesquière's futuristic aesthetic. Forensically choreographed, the gong of the Fondation Louis Vuitton announced the commencement of the show just before sunset. The models emerged from the house and circled the pool to a soundtrack played through Plexiglas towers of speakers, as the audience watched from low stools and a drone captured live-stream footage from overhead.

LOUIS VUITTON

2016 Cruise, California

LOUIS VUITTON

Autumn/Winter 2016 Menswear, Paris

This collection, entitled 'Future Heritage', was
a tribute to Paris in the face of the horrific
events of 13 November 2015. The show was
scheduled to allow the glow of the sun into the
venue in order to perfectly frame artist Shinji
Ohmaki's cloud-like installation, which softly
rippled above the catwalk.

MAISON MARGIELA

Spring/Summer 2013 Ready-to-Wear, Paris

The concept of this set was to make guests feel like they were seeing the world from the inside of a plastic bag – a space under construction, a work in progress. Designers at Maison Margiela wrapped the entire interior of the Hôtel Salomon de Rothschild with plastic, even installing special ventilation so as to avoid any risk of suffocation. Hints of Dadaist, Japanese and sci-fi influences were evident in the collection itself.

Though designer John Galliano refused to give interviews at the time, his collection appeared to be inspired by an eclectic mix of 1950s daywear, *Bride of Frankenstein* and Japanese geishas. Above the audience, tightly packed rows of spotlights elevated at alternating heights created bright patterns that reflected on the sheet-metal runway. This modern, clinical structure created a jarring contrast with the classic frescoed walls that embraced the set.

MAISON MARGIELA

Spring/Summer 2016 Ready-to-Wear, Paris

MARC JACOBS

Spring/Summer 2007 Ready-to-Wear, New York

This set featured a backdrop of rolling hills
behind an asymmetrical catwalk that was
painted green. The angled runway was elevated
over a sea-like core filled with blue sweets.
The mock-bucolic set was designed by Stefan
Beckman, and the collection had a whimsical
flavour, with wide hems, bandanas and baggy
sleeves all featuring.

MARC JACOBS

Autumn/Winter 2014 Ready-to-Wear, New York

For this show, Jacobs took us to his fashion dreamland. The low-hanging tactile clouds set the scene for a soft and serene collection, but as the show progressed, they took on a heavier sense as their shadows played on the pale models, and the repetitive soundtrack – a spoken-word version of 'Happy Days are Here Again' performed by Jessica Lange – cast a soporific spell over the audience. Jacobs stated that his inspiration was women who have strength without aggression, and this set, by collaborator Stefan Beckman, encapsulated this sense of calm confidence.

MARC JACOBS

Spring/Summer 2015 Ready-to-Wear, New York

Inspired by a 1976 avant-garde short film called *The Girl Chewing Gum*, this season Jacobs decided to create an art piece that each spectator could make their own. Citing *The Wizard of Oz* as another reference, he turned again to Stefan Beckman who created the hot-pink set of an otherwise everyday suburban house with matching gravel. The spectacle was transformed into a completely immersive experience with the addition of headphones for every guest, which were provided by Beats by Dre. When worn, these blocked out all background noise and played a soothing computer-generated voice that narrated the scene, created by another Jacobs collaborator, music producer Steve Mackey.

MARY KATRANTZOU

Spring/Summer 2012 Ready-to-Wear, London

'Man meets machine meets nature' was the idea behind Mary Katrantzou's SS12 presentation, and the collection plaited these traditional antagonists into a coherent theme. The prints – featuring metallic sheens, delicate petals, car parts, tin cans, feathers and scales – reflected both the machine-like nature of industrial production and the vitality of Mother Earth. The set was made up of blocks of carnations coloured red, pink, yellow and white, and this uniformity and vibrant repetition was evident in the collection itself.

For this collection, inspiration was drawn from classic Hollywood archetypes – cowboys, princesses and young lovers – fused together to create unique individual pieces displayed against a cinematic backdrop. Visual references were key, with films such as *Romeo + Juliet*, *Wild at Heart* and *Natural Born Killers* all telling the same tale – of love and love lost. This duality was reflected by the mirror-like set, which was created by Bureau Betak and featured a foil-covered catwalk surrounded by silver balloons

MARY KATRANTZOU

Autumn/Winter 2016 Ready-to-Wear, London

MIU MIU

Autumn/Winter 2013 Ready-to-Wear, Paris

Rem Koolhaas and AMO took on the task of converting the Palais d'Iéna into a dedicated runway for Paris Fashion Week. The room was shrunk down into an isolated layer by inserting a lowered ceiling and a raised floor. These black grates, corralled by pale columns, served to create a controlled and almost claustrophobic set for the audience. To the sound of the Eurythmics' classic 'The City Never Sleeps', models walked demurely in long, lean cuts that were punctuated by polka dots and brightly coloured handbags and accessories.

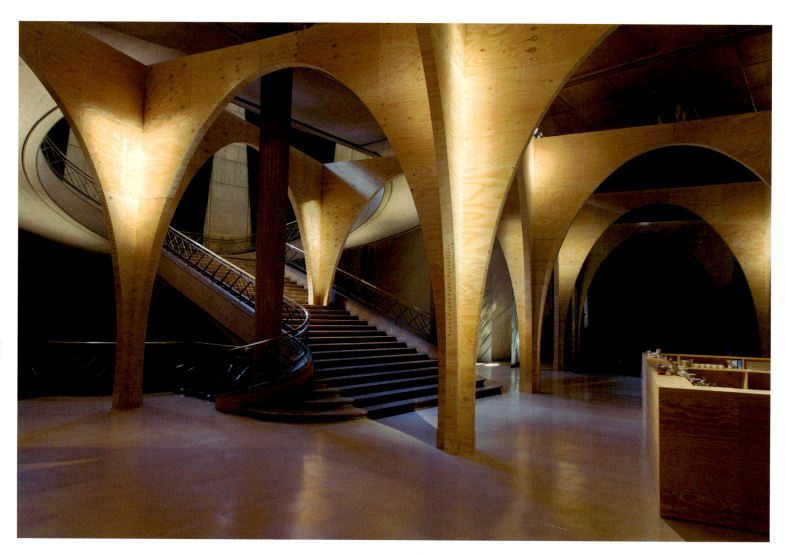

MIU MIU

Spring/Summer 2015 Ready-to-Wear, Paris

The set of Miu Miu's SS15 catwalk show, designed by AMO, was a surprise even to even to Miuccia Prada herself: 'I did not know they were designing this, and it is perfect!' Reimagining the interior of Auguste Perret's Palais d'Iéna, plywood arches evoked an old Protestant church as guests were placed in uncomfortable seats as if praying for forgiveness. The collection featured rebellious looks with a stroppy, punk attitude in luscious fabrics like handwoven silk jacquard.

The historic Palazzo del Senato was transformed into a life-sized boxing arena under the direction of designer Thom Browne and producer Etienne Russo. Four boxers and an adjudicator entered the ring and glared imposingly down as male and female models wearing red, white and black paraded in front of the crowd. The collection pulled inspiration from the world of boxing, with hooded robes, glove stitching and padded blazers all featuring. The sportswear-inspired clothing was combined with traditional tailoring to create a blend of functional and athletic pieces.

MONCLER

Spring/Summer 2015 Gamme Bleu, Milan

MONCLER

Spring/Summer 2016 Gamme Bleu, Milan

The sport of competitive rowing provided the inspiration for Moncler's SS16 collection, and the set, in the Padiglione Visconti, was again the brainchild of Etienne Russo. At the centre of the stage lay two wooden racing boats with full sets of oars, seemingly fresh from a Cambridge or Oxford university event. Reds, whites, blues and pinstripes made up the majority of the collection, with cuts that complemented the sleek outline of the boats. Four separate teams of rowers entered the room in colour-coded athletic wear, sporting trench coats, cardigans, polo shirts, fisherman hats, shorts and knee-high socks. The models then gathered in huddles to discuss strategy and complete the illusion of a collegiate sports meet.

Inspired by the 1990s, an enormous retro stereo was the end point of the catwalk for this collection of New York City-style streetwear. Colourful and energetic, the outfits featured strong outlines, cuts and defined volumes, as well as prints inspired by American graffiti. The set was designed by Random Productions, and from the models' accessories to the giant boombox, everything was XXL.

MOSCHINO

Autumn/Winter 2015 Ready-to-Wear, Milan

MULBERRY

Autumn/Winter 2016 Ready-to-Wear, London

This Mulberry show took place at the Guildhall in London, with a set recreating the interior of a Gothic church. New creative director Johnny Coca captured the brand's English streetwear heritage, transforming the looks in a modern way with graphic touches, pop-colour fishnets and nods to punk culture.

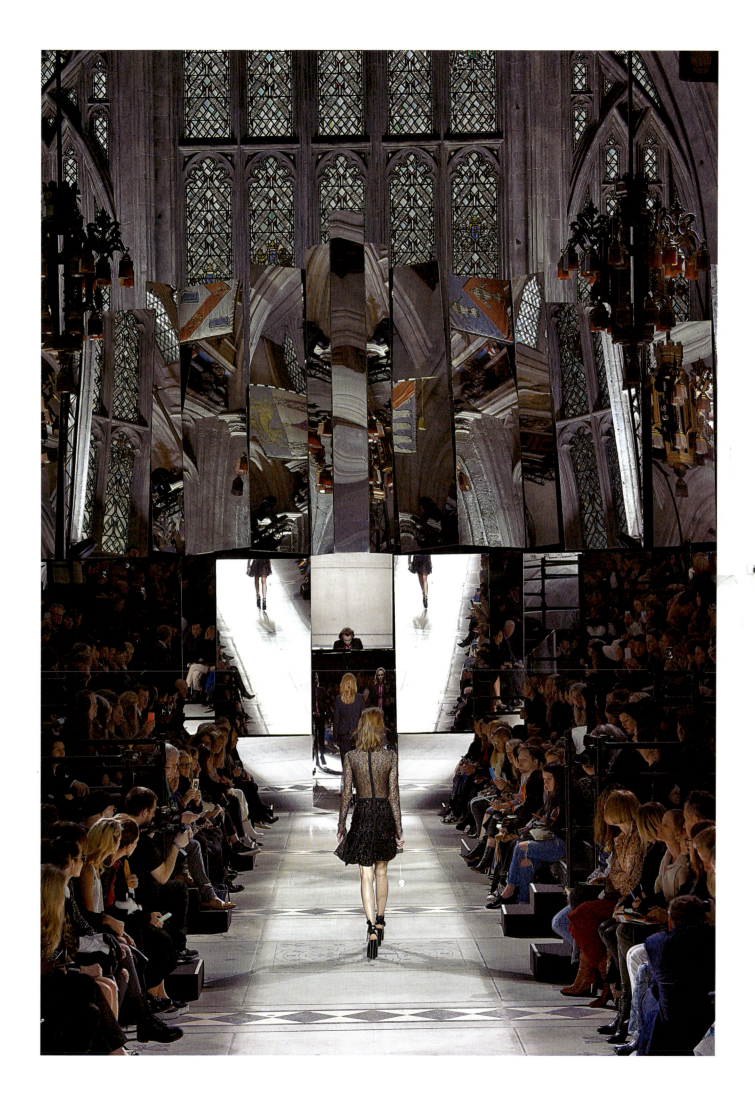

PETER PILOTTO

Spring/Summer 2013 Ready-to-Wear, London

This Peter Pilotto collection was an explosion
of dazzling graphics. A U-shaped runway
covered with digital prints was laid down by
designers Christopher de Vos and Peter Pilotto.
Illuminated by fluorescent lights, and with
inspiration drawn from Italian frescoes, the
collection was all about texture and pattern.

PHILLIP LIM

Spring/Summer 2016 Ready-to-Wear, New York

Calling on architectural artist Maya Lin to
create this set, Phillip Lim invited the audience
to 'stop and smell the flowers'. Models walked
around triangular mounds of dirt placed in
the Feng Shui tradition in the barren industrial
space. A collection of floral footwear, matching
embroidered silk shirts and earth-toned dresses
echoed the dramatic surroundings.

PHILIPP PLEIN

Autumn/Winter 2015 Ready-to-Wear, Milan

An enormous roller coaster was the centrepiece for this Philipp Plein show in Milan's historic Palazzo delle Scintille. The empty carriages whirled around the huge, triangular catwalk, illuminated by LED spotlights. The monochrome colours of the roller coaster were reflected in the clothing, which featured variations on the theme of streetwear. American singer Azealia Banks opened the show, lit by the neon glare of a giant #pleinwarriors sign.

PHILIPP PLEIN

Spring/Summer 2016 Menswear, Milan

The centre of this dramatic gold and silver space was lined with a row of burnt-out vehicle wreckage. Bikers, monster trucks and flaming cars zoomed up and down the set, jumping ramps and performing stunts, before the models emerged in a collection featuring ripped shirts, biker jackets and super-skinny pants.

Pierre Cardin's SS08 collection, composed of 200 designs, was held in the vast desert surrounding the Whistling Sand Mountain along the well-known Silk Road in north-west China's Gansu Province. The theme for this huge undertaking was 'Marco Polo', and it certainly evoked the sense of wonder of a European traveller to the East. Models appeared from behind a dune and snaked along a 280-metre runway laid out across the sand. At the climax of the show, a model in a wedding dress emerged on a camel, just as the setting sun turned the entire scene purple.

PIERRE CARDIN

Spring/Summer 2008 Ready-to-Wear, Gansu

PRADA

Spring/Summer 2012 Menswear, Milan

For this menswear collection, Prada turned to something she admittedly hates as a source of inspiration: the world of golf. Setting the stage with green Astroturf, and seating guests on rows of sky-blue cubes throughout the space, the catwalk was transformed into an indoor golf course. Models wove through the seats wearing checked shorts, double-breasted jackets, floral scarves and brightly coloured caps, accompanied by cowboy boots and jewelled golf shoes.

PRADA

Spring/Summer 2014 Ready-to-Wear, Milan

The venue for this Prada show was outfitted by a team of mural artists with images and messages that echoed Miuccia Prada's own political and social activist roots. 'I want to inspire women to struggle,' she proclaimed. Depicting visions of womanhood, 1990s Riot grrrls and South American and Mexican political street art, the artwork was reflected on the garments. The collection featured artistically pieced-together prints, knits and colourful furs in clashing patterns, styled with tube socks and sandals.

PRADA

Spring/Summer 2015 Ready-to-Wear, Milan

Designed by frequent Prada collaborators AMO, the Via Fogazzaro space in Milan was transformed with a rust-coloured carpet onto which purple sand cascaded from tall piles. The clothes reflected classic luxury fabrics and prints such damask, flocking and brocades custom-created for the collection.

Set in an industrial space decked out with metal floors and ceilings, this Prada menswear collection also featured female models. A written manifesto was placed on each guest's seat, proclaiming 'gender is a context and context is often gendered'. Walking to a soundtrack produced by Frédéric Sanchez, male and female models shared the quartz-infused runway space in clothes that played with gender tropes.

Autumn/Winter 2015 Menswear, Milan

In the beautiful setting of the Villa La Petraia in Florence, the American creative duo of Jack McCollough and Lazaro Hernandez presented their collection as special guests of Pitti W. Eschewing the conventional fashion show, they collaborated with three artists to create a video, an installation, and a live performance. The project was carried out in association with New York's Art Production Fund, who introduced the designers to video artist Kalup Linzy, performance artist Kembra Pfahler and installation artist Haim Steinbach. Steinbach installed a pristine white carpet in the villa's stunning Renaissance courtyard to display the collection's accessories.

PROENZA SCHOULER

Pre-Spring/Summer 2010 Ready-to-Wear, Florence

RALPH & RUSSO

Spring/Summer 2015 Couture, Paris

Florals and colours straight out of a curated English garden were the theme at London-based Ralph & Russo's show. The set was composed of a cream-coloured runway marked by columns in hues as soft and dreamy as the princess-like gowns themselves. With barely-there pastel ruffles, organza *degradés* and ornate embroidery, each piece catered to couture aficionados eager to scoop up their next piece from the brand's third collection, deemed their strongest to date.

ROBERTO CAVALLI

Spring/Summer 2011 Ready-to-Wear, Milan

Situated in a greenhouse specially erected beneath Napoleon's Arco della Pace in central Milan, Cavalli's SS11 show was the epitome of the *maison*'s excessively lavish style. Huge glossy plants towered over a faux-suede runway as a tribe of models paraded in snakeskin patterns and tasselled fabrics – a primitive but genetically gifted tribe in a glamorous jungle.

Opening the show in total darkness, with guests seated around a shallow pond, Cavalli turned up the heat as a ring of fire burst from the floor accompanied by a co-ordinated display of blue spotlights. The scene was perfectly set for a collection marrying wild elements with 1920s glamour; alongside fire-hued signature Cavalli animal prints and long furs, there were sinuous black dresses trimmed with glowing flame patterns.

ROBERTO CAVALLI

Autumn/Winter 2014 Ready-to-Wear, Milan

SAINT LAURENT

Autumn/Winter 2016 Menswear, Los Angeles

Hedi Slimane chose to present his Saint Laurent men's autumn collection and 'Part 1' of the women's pre-autumn collection at the storied Hollywood Palladium on Sunset Boulevard, and the experience was an homage to the designer's adopted city and its dynamic music scene. The glamourous 1940s room was interjected by a moving light installation, as models took to the runway in vintage-inspired looks that channelled David Bowie and Jimi Hendrix. Following the show, the A-list audience was treated to performances from eleven musical acts, including Father John Misty, Beck and Joan Jett.

SCHIAPARELLI

Spring/Summer 2015 Couture, Paris

Schiaparelli's SS15 collection was held in the Place Vendôme, on a set commissioned by Farida Khelfa, ambassador of the *maison*, and designed by photographer Jean-Paul Goude. The brand was at that time transitioning between designers, and so the show, its environment completely immersed in pink, was a tribute to Elsa Schiaparelli. Guests sat on long benches in the middle of the room to admire a varied collection, the impact of each look enhanced by the intensity of the monochromatic set. Performers from Les Chérubins choir sang from the upper windows, a tribute to Elsa's enthusiasm for incorporating live performance into her shows.

TOMMY HILFIGER

Autumn/Winter 2012 Ready-to-Wear, New York

In this show, designed by OBO's René Célestin and Susan Schroeder, Tommy Hilfiger brought town and country together, as the audience walked through a grand gate to find themselves in a quintessential city park, with those in the front row sitting on real park benches surrounded by trees and ivy. The designer stated that the collection was designed for a girl 'as much at ease at the hunt club as she is on Park Avenue', and its nods to the 1960s were enhanced by a relaxing soundtrack of Simon & Garfunkel.

TOMMY HILFIGER

Spring/Summer 2015 Ready-to-Wear, New York

With a collection inspired by rock music and festival culture, it's no wonder this Tommy Hilfiger show was staged to make the viewers feel like they had been catapulted into a music festival. Set designer Randall Peacock, with the creative input of Julie Mannion, decked out the Park Avenue Armory with a large lawn decorated with a huge psychedelic floral star, with musical instruments placed in the garden and guests seated along the perimeter.

Building on a reputation for stellar fashion shows and commitment to a theme, Tommy Hilfiger planted a huge ocean liner inside the Park Avenue Armory to unveil a collection bursting with new twists on familiar nautical motifs. As the *TH Atlantic*'s funnels pumped steam out against a starry backdrop, VIPs watched from seats on the deck, the maximalist setting a perfect complement to the playful collection.

TOMMY HILFIGER

Autumn/Winter 2016 Ready-to-Wear, New York

VALENTINO

Autumn/Winter 2013 Couture, Paris

For this Couture collection, designers Maria Grazia Chiuri and Pierpaolo Piccioli were inspired by the treasures that are to be discovered in museums and in cabinets of curiosities, where every item is unique and original, but at the same time connected to all the others. The catwalk was a very long piece of exquisite grey fabric, echoing the mottling of the walls, which were in turn embedded with precious heirlooms, providing the perfect backdrop to the style of the clothes, inspired by a distant epoch of opulence and fine art.

VERSACE

Autumn/Winter 2016 Menswear, Milan

'I'm thinking of the future. This is the ultimate expression of the future: space.' Donatella Versace's AW16 menswear collection was a space-age take on sportswear, and the set design was suitably futuristic. The immaculate white space, with its atmospheric purple and blue lighting, called to mind cinema's iconic spaceships and complemented the high-shine metallics and ice-white fabrics of the collection.

VIKTOR & ROLF

Autumn/Winter 2015 Couture, Paris

Viktor Horsting and Rolf Snoeren are continually interested in the question of whether fashion is an art form, and so they presented their AW15 Couture collection, 'Wearable Art', in a gallery at the Palais de Tokyo. The pieces, featuring hinged frames, seemed to have been taken down from the gallery walls and melded to the models' forms. During the show, the designers became performance artists, removing some of the models' outfits to hang them back on the walls; a complex achievement in the short show time, and one that piqued the interest of art collectors, further blurring the line between fashion and art.

VIONNET

Autumn/Winter 2014 Ready-to-Wear, Paris

Architectural white screens were softened by both transparent and gothic suggestions in this set design, with white tulips on the runway and origami shapes hanging from the rafters. The romantic atmosphere, where nature and architecture played as if in the moonlight, was the perfect set to enhance the collection's fluid yet assertive designs.

VIONNET

Spring/Summer 2015 Ready-to-Wear, Paris

Vionnet's SS15 collection, presented at the Cité de l'Architecture et du Patrimoine, was inspired by ballet and by the work of Piero Manzoni, a radical and controversial Italian artist who died in 1963 aged just twenty-nine. The silhouettes were Amazonian; the dresses, worn with oversized backpacks and woven sandals that climbed up the leg like tree bark, were finished with warrior-style belts that echoed Manzoni's famous eggs. In contrast, the long runway was spare, and the models walked in a brisk and business-like fashion under a discreet row of overhead lights.

Westwood called this collection 'Mirror the World', and the staging certainly mirrored the fashion icon's political and environmental activism. In a dark basement space (whose signage advertised an 'Alien Sex Club'), models in paper crowns with dirty faces carried signs protesting fracking, global warming, and the controversial TTIP agreement, to an oppressive soundtrack of sirens. Against this stirring political backdrop, the nature-inspired collection was sophisticated and robust, designed for a woman of substance who appreciates her place in the world. As Westwood reflected, 'You're very beautiful because you understand the beauty of the world and you understand the human race and you want to do your best.'

VIVIENNE WESTWOOD

Spring/Summer 2016 Red Label Ready-to-Wear, London

PHOTOGRAPHY CREDITS

222

223

Acknowledgements

We would like to deeply thank all the *maisons*, designers, press offices, production agencies, photographers and architects who contributed to this book:

Agency V; Alexander McQueen; Alexander Wang; AMO/OMA; Anna Sui; Antonio Marras; Anya Hindmarch; Barbieri & Ridet; BOSS; Bureau Betak; Céline; Chanel; Christian Dior; Dior Homme; Dolce & Gabbana; Dries Van Noten; Dsquared2; Elie Saab; Emanuela Schmeidler Press Office; Erdem; Ermenegildo Zegna; Etro; Eyesight; Fendi; Givenchy; Gucci; Henrik Vibskov; Hunter Original; Iris van Herpen; Jean Paul Gaultier; John Galliano; Karla Otto Press Offices; Kenzo; Lanvin; Louis Vuitton; Maison Margiela; Marc Jacobs; Mary Katrantzou; Miu Miu; Moncler; Moschino; Mulberry; Negri Firman Press Office, Phillip Lim; Philipp Plein; Pierre Cardin; Pitti Immagine; Prada; Proenza Schouler; Ralph & Russo; Roberto Cavalli; Saint Laurent; Schiaparelli; The Communication Store; Tommy Hilfiger; Valentino; Versace; Viktor & Rolf; Villa Eugénie; Vionnet; Vivienne Westwood.

A very special thanks to Colin McDowell and Diane Pernet for joining the project.

Thanks also to YO Fashion & Luxury Events, Orsola Amadeo, Giacomo Alberto Vieri and all our colleagues who helped us during this journey.

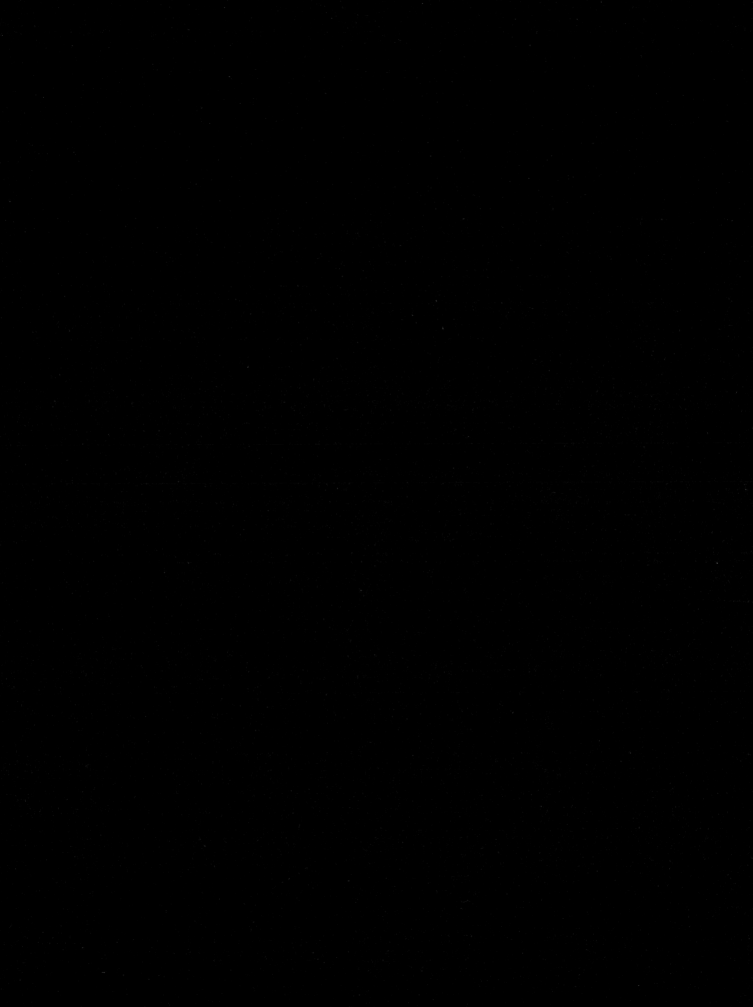